In a Woman's Skin

Susan Flynn

Swan Press

Swan Press
32 Joy Street
Dublin 4
D04 HN22

ISBN: 978-0-9933415-8-8

Photographs by Susan Flynn

Design and Layout by Lia Media
liamedia15@gmail.com
Mobile: 087 24 29 586

Printed in Ireland

Dedicated to Margaret, with love

hair flying –
the supple hazel branches
best for riding winds

Acknowledgements

Acknowledgements to publications in which some of these poems have appeared:

Prose on a Bed of Rhyme – Swan Press, 2012:
Greyhound; International Fiction and Poetry
Chapbook Competition Anthology – Doire Press, 2013:
Heterodoxy; Beneath the Clock – Swan Press, 2019:
*The Moylough Belt Shrine, Cosmic Time, Whisper Your
Secrets.*

Thanks to:

Eithne Cavanagh for editorial assistance
Gavin Cobbe for computer rescues
Mary Guckian and Swan Press
Friends in Rathmines Writers' Workshop

CONTENTS

Part 1

Part 2

Part 3

Part 6

Part 7

In a Woman's Skin

Part 1

GREETINGS

Twisting the wireless dial from town to town,
I'd rather crackly fizz between the stations
to all the humdrum chatter; I like it because
of the notion of remnant cosmic microwaves
pulsing at my eardrums from the beginning
of everything (thirteen point seven billion years,
give or take a few yoctoseconds) – the bang.

And some time, aeons past imagining,
Voyager's Golden Record might bump beings
in Ophiuchus or Andromeda or beyond,
then thunder, surf, whale and birdsong, sawing,
music and greetings, voiced from a blue dot,
might cause some little membranes to vibrate,
tissues might shiver, change colour, and contract.

Or maybe these life forms, if more than blobs of
    mucus,
will lift the stylus with opposable thumbs
and lay it on the grooves, sense the noise,
wave feathered antennae, waft forth pheromones,
pluck at stridulatory combs on their legs –
or else – intuit the unsaid in good will words,
shake their wise heads, close thin green lips. For
    good.

WHISPER YOUR SECRETS

We moss embossed stone pigs
are more than your glance perceives:
all the bits and pieces
of myriad lives, snowing
carbon confetti upon
the ocean floor – wishes,
worries, doubts, faiths,
sublime epiphanies –
trickled in flickering sunlight
down, down, fondled
by fronds of laminaria,
chancing off corals, noticed,
allowed pass by, to dance,
drift and lie for good
on earth's silty breast.

Embedded safe in limestone,
quarried, carried off, sculpted
in forms familiar to you
three hundred million years on
(a blink of your god's eye)
to please your visual and haptic
senses.
          Press your mouth
to our cold ears, whisper –
your secrets are safe with us.

LICKING THE MOON

Stones from a tumbled wall
lie near a moon pool
in the heart of woody tangle.

A fox's curled tongue
licks the creamy comma,
light trembling a little.

PARABOLA

Folding my little bamboo
craft with closely inscribed
words from the heart,
I tamp it well in the muzzle
of a cannon aiming East
at tonight's full moon;
I light the fizzing fuse,
my origami spaceship
whizzes its ordained
parabolic orbit.

Some time before dawn
I dream of radiant
illusions, out of reach;
I believe my craft
wafts to white dust
away in the Bay of Rainbows
sprinkling my words,
a life in haiku
relinquished to the man
on the moon for safe holding.

MESSENGER

Unfolding the origami of my bones,
the pains of garden labour hammer knees
and neck, the left latissimus dorsi strained
by dibbling ground with pelvis splayed and
    flexed,
head dangled down – I'm thinking of a giraffe,
her limbs akimbo drinking at a waterhole.
I roll my shoulders, cast the eyes back to when
tasks were done faster, heft of boulders disdained.

But robin alights on the birdbath by my side,
excites his olive feathers, sprinkles a shower
of shimmering droplets; a bower of apple
    blossoms
and bluebells make his stage. The sunlight in
his eye gives the instruction I require:
to gather breath, to see things just as they are.

HAPPY HUNTING GROUNDS

I've mislaid another word –
for a *specialist agriculture* –

So I'm out here on my knees
rooting down in wet clay
for my lost word, and hopeful –
often they're deep underground
where fingers push the rich

soil in which I mixed
manure and strips of kelp
our winter gales gifted –
furbelows, dabberlocks,
poor man's weatherglass.

Worms twist, millipedes ball
themselves in astonishment,
I feel I'm drawing closer,
black to my happy elbows:
it's 'hydrowhatchamacallit'.

The earth smells luscious,
a gust shivers the lilac
sprinkling me with drops,
I pull my fingers up:
'hydroponics' in my palms.

DELVE DEEP

You'd need to get down on your knees,
Open your eyes to the bog
To see beyond a vast
Quilt of black and brown
Glanced on, hastening past;
So, wet your arms and legs,
Discover red and yellow
Sticky glinting sundew,
Blowing ceannabawns,
Four pale eggs of curlew,
Verdigris lichen mats,
Scarlet elf cups,
Blue butterwort,
Bog myrtle, asphodels –
Spiders, shiny beetles,
Emperor moths' silk webs
Wrapping purple ling,
A chandelier of dew –

And you could push your arms
Beneath the spongy sphagnum,
Your nails tough as backhoes
On turf cutting machines,
Then deeper, darker, denser
Your hands could rummage roots,
Stumps of ancient pine,
Diluvian leaves and pollen –
Touch a cold bronze cauldron,
A wooden churn of butter,
Cache or votive offering;

Finger a torc of gold,
Unearth a sad brown king
Noosed in plaited willow,
His jaw fallen open
Like an untold grief –
Or, some psalter of vellum,
Papyrus, leather and horn
Shovelled out in a bucket
Like a brown mud pie,
Calligraphic stew
Ushered into light
From a vale of tears,
Twelve hundred buried years.

TRUST

Fist sized knots of worms, pink and squirming,
  greet
This morning's tipped leavings, peels, egg shells,
  tea;
The worms are blessed and thanked for labour,
  all the bounty
They process for the earth, her poor ailing soil;
Beautiful they are, with their intrinsic worth.
Each takes sufficiency and gives for the good of
  all
In quiet coexistence, no need for potentate.
It seems Republic of Compost, ungoverned,
  works on trust.

The Power that made the worm made me; we
  both love life.
I tip the slippery dwellers in from the perilous
  border,
Recap dark silence and spade their gift on the
  ground,
Brown, clean, crumbly nourishment for the land.
Minerals in slow time are sucked up by spinach
Which, well enriched by worms' leavings, comes
  to table.

THE MOYLOUGH BELT SHRINE

When a tent is folded
Do whispers hang around
Wafting in the dunes?

Does the pale rectangle
Where sleepers pressed the machair
Contain their energy?

What about shadows,
Do they snag on furze bushes
When their owners leave?

Where went the power
When the man with amazing
Hands passed on?

At his final sigh
Did healing push out,
Expand to the sky

Or soak into bog
To be held by earth,
And fed to roots and feet?

When Towey's sleán, slicing
The dark turves cleanly
Met with metal, what

Unsayable essence
Ringed within a belt
Made him catch his breath?

LOOK BACK

Dead Man's Walk wends from gaol to Gallows
   Hill.
Idyllic pastures hold a groove of grief.
Now, children from the school plant daffodils,
And cover layers of history with leafy
Hope. They scatter meadow seeds for bees
And hang 'leave only footprints' signs on trees.

Brambles and whitethorn fringe the narrow track.
Beyond a ruined church, the only bend,
Where the condemned in shackles might look
   back;
Above the taunts of gangs, might hear a wren
Lamenting from a branch on that old oak,
Three hundred years a witness in the glen
To bands of men, who toiled with wood and rope,
To souls who shuffled up their final slope.

Part 2

winter sunset
lichens in the birch wood
let go of light drops

OCTOBER DANCE

The white haired woman walks alone to the
  wood.
At dusk, her stooped form can be spied from
  here,
through branches spilling saffron and rusty
  leaves.
She waves her twig-like arms, palms tilted up,
chin poking forward, shuffling her limbs, she
    sways
in ebb and flow, revolves her bent old trunk,
makes rapid flounces, scuffing dry beech mast,
and claps her hands or plucks at air, or ghosts.
Still the gold leaves drift on the wings of wind,
wafting on air puffs, twisting, missing her grasps.
'Oh' and 'oh' she whines, while the fall wheels
    past
her weird dance, until the tempo wavers,
her arms sink to her sides, the head nods down.

SAMHAIN

Who are those wild hags
tilting up their chins
and laughing, arms outspread,
leaping to grab at leaves
all showering down at once,
gold tumbling from blue sky?

Into the darker wood
all pad without a word,
sniffing at scoops of mulch,
fingering furry mosses,
pocketing fungus fruits,
eyeing dyes for cloths –

verdigris lichen, stag's horn,
jew's ear, purple toadstools,
candlesnuff, weeping widow,
woolly boot, scarlet elf cup,
King Alfred's cramp balls,
club foot, witch's butter –

out to the airy clearing
where Samhain will be hailed;
so, barefoot in a circle
they dance on dewy grasses
waving wide winged sleeves,
those ululating hags,

dancing for frost and death
and the long wait for the sun

'til mist shrouds the ground
up to their scaly knees,
song is changed to croaks
and black crows scatter round.

SOLSTICE

A big sky spreads above reedy fields. Looking back, the east is inky. Ahead, violet and lemon streaks linger; the red sun sank a while ago behind hills south west of here.
Blanketed horses pull hay from a bale behind a lopsided gate tied with twine; their hot nostril breaths smoke icy air. Soon all is shadow on shadow. Somewhere a cow bellows continuously.

rooks on a bare ash –
cattle low at milking hour
gathering in time

Grass crunches in the middle of the potholed lane. The new moon is too thin to be a guide, so it is necessary to grope stone walls crisped with lichens, count remaining gates and turn for home by the scratchy blackthorn. Nearby, a sheep coughs like a man. Creatures huddled behind bare bushes smell of comfort.

new moon reposes
in frozen cattle puddles
a creamy comma

ADVENT

A rainbow shone, and sure enough
there followed showers and then the sun
sank down behind the Wicklow hills;
and now beneath crepuscular
grey clouds and ivied trees I stand.

I relish pre-roost fluted notes
of long-tailed tits and hidden thrush.

Between the branches, yellow light
shines out from stained-glass windows; now
I hear the antiphons of old –
"O come O come, Emmanuel"
in muffled tones through stones and glass.

On Murphy's hill a donkey 'mourns
in lonely exile here', at dusk.

In five days, winter solstice comes,
but even now the drops of rain
in rows on ash twigs magnify
what light remains, and on I pace
in time with chants: "Rejoice! Rejoice!"

SOLSTICES IN THE YEAR 2020

Summer

The equinox rolled by, oak buds unwrapped
before the ash – fine summer almost certain.
Easter, if it occurred, was etched upon
the face of a grey haired woman pushing a
      curtain.
Outside, we sidled like knights on a vast chess
      board
exchanging embarrassed smiles behind our
      scarves,
turning our faces away or crossing roads,
a sign of disrespect in our real lives.
Yet kindnesses and acts of love were sprinkled
on friend and stranger; these will be remembered.
The swifts and swallows came, and squealing
      terns
Built nests as always, and increased their
      numbers.
By solstice, daffodils had shrunk away
and sunset pastels soothed the long, long day.

Winter

A fan of fading sunlight fingers clouds
as day retreats, surrendering to shade
soft brushing mountains paling to the west,
and garden tasks are quietly put aside.
Frost crisps the glistening grass, makes plume of
      breath,

the longest night lit faintly by moonbeams;
the creatures, understanding seasons' rhythms,
accept, and torpid, yield to sleep and dreams.
Bats wrap their slumber in their soft black wings,
cocoons of moths hang still in hollow trees,
birds push their innocent heads deep in warm
     down,
curled hedgehogs breathe in silent piles of leaves.
Then hour by hour this darkest night wheels on,
until the bottom of the sky turns crimson.

CENTRIFUGAL

Maybe their backs
feel breezes fanned
from farewell waves
at the ferry port
but their faces turn
to far horizons

and even the moon
as it sweeps its ellipse,
slips away from us
one and a half
inches each year;
we ought to notice
as this is the rate
our fingernails grow;
we snip or nibble
or file them and if
I had neglected
to trim my nails
from the beginning
today they would reach
seven foot six –

I would surely need
a band of attendants
for my scrolls of keratin
looping their orbits
around like spirals
in a nautilus shell
or a coiled pot

or a spiral galaxy,
the curls widening at every turn
stretching away
from the hub of things.

GENTIANA VERNA

Centrifugal – white stigma
encircled by five lemony stamens
within five petals, Athena's eyes
made of sky where Alps meet
Mediterranean and Arctic ice,
chiming limestone resounding
with enthusiasms of skylarks
up somewhere in that blue space
particular to late afternoon,
where soon, in inky void,
cold constellations will sweep their arc
in infinite space-time, mirrors of these
gentians starring grass, here,
by the Caher river, best adored
by lying prone on damp ground
with a hand lens bringing the creamy
stigma star closer to your eye.

POLLYBLOBS
(or Caltha calustris for botanists)

Apt epithet for golden globes
shouting their brightness from shady green
glossy leaves, heart-shaped for love.

Nestled in spongy, undrained places,
opened corollas of five or six petals
surpass buttercup and crocus yellows.

Not made to delight us! Our generation
resists snapping fat purple stems,
leaves the marsh marigolds in their place.

The unopened ones are paler balls,
water-bubbles, baubles for fairies:
wait for it, they seem to whisper,

tomorrow or the next day, we too
shall amaze you; our buttery lambency
will halt your squelching fen footfall.

Part 3

no need for mirrors –
lying on new mown hay
in my dog's gaze

RAINBOWS

Spinning her orb last night,
the spider could not have planned
for the light of dawn to reveal
myriad shimmering hues
on every silken line;

she could not have imagined
the joy she would gift to one
who, flinging open curtains
on a window facing east,
sees her own world less common.

The silk reflects, refracts,
scatters light in rainbows
spanning Heaven and Earth.
The blessing of the gift –
it is brief, and ungraspable.

AFTER ALL

The house subsides, sinks,
stinks, slime menaces
the hall, mould and grime
film window and wall,
black humps of fungus
emboss crumbling mortar,
woodworm laces joists,
blisters bulge plaster
like foetid sores, floors
groan under water.

Yet booklice thread lives,
thriving generations
eat Mrs Beeton,
or emerge from Exodus
as free as silverfish,
like slivers of mercury
gliding in pale light,
a coin of moon reflected
from a fly-spotted mirror
with peeling gilded balls.

Mice nest in a press;
spiders court at the pace
of a clock's hour hand;
beneath a curled veneer
an earwig mothers her young.

Bats shadow the attic,
blinking sequin eyes.
A skulk of foxes pads
thin trails in dewy weeds.
All is well, after all.

THIS HOME

for the patient spider in her small corner
the wasps who stream in below the floorboards
the moth larvae nourished by darned woollens
the ants yearly polishing nuptial wings
the grasshopper strumming his thighs with hope
the mice dancing reels on ceiling boards
the hedgehogs who root in the foxes' supper
the squirrels who visit the peanut feeders
the zen-like frogs with their pinhole nostrils
the myriad worms in microbial earth
the blackbird, first to sing before dawn
the robin, light as a thought on my finger
the buzzards whose squeals claim the blue vault
the dogs past and present guarding this space

with permeable edges and walls with holes
we all pass through, for our own spell
leaving skin flakes and fragrances
our stories, dreams and energies
like salt on the breeze, like thunder of waves

GREYHOUND

You say - a black greyhound.
Fact - except for a spark
of white on the muscular chest
and the toes, they too are white.
But when the sun is high
and he nudges his needle head
into your soft centre,
you lay your face on his back,
on the powerful shoulder blades
and ridge of vertebrae
stretching to massive thighs,
then you perceive rainbows -
reds, greens, iridescent
on his every loved hair.

SIGNS

Dog throws back his head
to yawn, but also to laugh.
Here is the roof of his mouth,
black, ridged and grooved,
bumping down to the throat.

Exciting pheromones
fizz through tiny holes
behind his fine incisors,
swirl up the avenue
to his emotional hub.

What insights he inhales!
Enchantment in his eyes,
comma-nostrils flared,
wet black nose to the sky,
mackerel clouds: change is coming.

SKULK

After midnight when last straggles of drunks
have navigated the lanes to their lairs
staggering, pissing, jettisoning chips
in foil trays – a sort of silence comes

out of chaos, good for star gazing
or waiting for small nocturnal happenings
like urban foxes, at first streaks of shadow,
imaginings bolting between parked cars –

pressed to a wall, privileged you watch
tussling cubs leap and lap in lamplight
but the vixen, vigilant with pricked up ears
is onto you, your scent perhaps, and hisses

so they vanish. They must hold distrust.
Look up again – Pegasus kicks his heels.

MOTORWAY PRAYER

My car draws level
with a reddish brown
mound by the kerb,
a twisted jumble
of limbs, no not limbs,
not a dead fox,
sleeves of a coat
in coils, redemptive
garbage, not
a dead fox this
time – thank you
thank you – let
paws pad safely –

and look – sprinkling
the grassy median –
dandelions and
blood-red poppies!

Part 4

fingers open –
the dog's ashes leap up
to greet the wind

MOTHER

The full moon's doleful eyes look down.
A road of light golds black wave tips,
shines the shell of the old turtle.

She leaves behind the liminal frill,
heaves uphill towards darker land,
scuffs loose sand, moulds a hole.

Her face tilts up to her lunar guide,
higher now, gilding tears from her eyes
while her eggs, white balls like satellites,

roll one by one down the soft hollow.
She covers her cargo deep with hope,
and follows the cycle year on year.

TEMPTATION

They would run in the sea for a swim by the light
    of the moon;
At low tide, barefooted they hurried across the
    damp sands.
They schemed to explain that the tide turned and
    they were marooned.

They spread out their rug in a hollow of
    sheltering dune,
And, laughing at green phosphorescence scuffed
    up in their dance,
They ran in the sea for a swim by the light of the
    moon.

Then darker and deeper they waded, a tidal surge
    soon
Unleashing mercurial currents to cover the
    strands;
The tide had come in, they would say, so the two
    were marooned.

The man felt impelled to swim out to a ravishing
    tune,
Now spellbound by honey tongued songs of
    marine ululants,
Out farther to sea, for a swim by the light of the
    moon.

She clutched at his heels, well aware of sea
    maidens who croon

To enrapture poor sailors, then cupping his ears
with her hands
She kicked with the tide which had turned so that
they were marooned.

She pulled her pale mesmerised lover back up to
their dune,
Now well beyond reach of the sea nymphs'
attempts to entrance.
They had run in the sea for a swim by the light of
the moon.
Next day they would say the tide turned, so that
they were marooned.

HERRING

Herring flash fusiform
in hundreds of thousands,
grey green gold silver
gaping, gill gashes open,
out of their element,
pressed in a net.

Consider this fish:
she loves her life,
the flash of light,
safety of the myriad
on six sides synchronised
in mercurial fleetness,
ocean fragrances,
swallows of plankton,
near stillness in dark
secret frond hides,
wild exuberance
at spawning time,
shedding her eggs
in the males' milt soup.

She expresses herself
by streaming bubbles
out of her anus,
reads bubble gossip
from herring friends
(intelligence
beyond our ken).

She knows nothing of
her kind founding cities,
or warring people's
fishing rights frictions.
Maybe she knew
her journey would end,
but not like this.

Unique herring, noticed,
essence beloved,
every shining scale.

COASTAL BLESSING

May sands sliding into your footprints be
symbols of change.

May you feel the dependability of tidal ebbs and
flows.

Standing at the fringe of the sea, may you
understand strangeness.

May breezes over mounds of kelp stir an obscure
yearning in you.

May ships on the horizon be reminders of
connectedness.

May you share the delight of a stranger who
invites you to wonder at clouds.

Just as the cliffs hold sand martens' nests, may
you be sustained.

May endurance be the lesson from a pebble
rolled in the arches of your hand.

May the face on the full moon foster in you
reverie.

May moonbeams on a dark swell shine as your
path of hope.

Watching the warp and weft of gulls, may you
feel fellowship with the unfree.

May you be energised by the brightness of foam
from breakers.

When your gaze meets the seal's wet eyes may
you be certain of kinship.

May your view on the expanse of water nourish
your introspection.

May the sound of a foghorn bring forth your pity.

May your focus mirror that of the returning Brent
geese.

May the lighthouse lead your thoughts to home.

May the little turnstones fussing at water's edge
make you keen eyed.

May a rainbow's iridescence astonish you now as
in your infancy.

A DEATH

At low tide, this heavy mound of seal,
her nostrils huge, then slitted, her flank rising
and falling as she pulled in each slow breath.
From lips of waves her companion kept his
    watch.

I fretted from the shade of human ken.
In her dissolution she had to be alone.
I hoped her body's senses shrank, that she
was moored in consciousness of innocence.

The waning moon passed over her. It rained.
The tide filled in, then left her bared again,
and now all signs of life were gone, but mirrored
in her moist eye, the light and dark of this world.

I sprinkle crumbs for birds, my offering
which I dedicate to this seal, dreaming free
through veils of furbelows and dabberlocks,
her fur dappled by light in cleansing waters.

SILENCED

You'd be all astray
but for the damp margin;
sea has faded out,
forms blur and melt
into utter whiteness

which erases rocks,
swirls across the tide line,
pushes up the hill,
world vapour-dissolved;
now you could be missing.

Gone the consolation,
drawn out bass signals
on days such as this,
or the deep sound could find you
in bed, you'd think of them,

those lonely mariners:
hear us on sea or land,
the foghorns used to call,
listen, pray for us
so we may not be alone.

Ireland's foghorns were silenced
on 11th January, 2011.

TONGUE

I roll one pebble around on my tongue.
It feels primeval, has travelled far.
I learn its solid spheroidity,
its cold saltiness. It tastes good.
Dropped in my crock, I lick a new stone
rougher and weightier than the first.

I savour the characteristics and spit.
And so it continues with oval stones
grey and smooth with stripes of white,
some with fossils, and polished quartz,
granite with baby mirrors of schist,
creamy brown flints – licked and retained.

I pick three or four from the wet tide line
which flick and rattle against incisors.
The beach presents a surfeit of pebbles
but my crock is filling, my tongue is gleaning
diameter, texture, unevenness.
One by one, I roll them around.

DRAWN

Down to land's limit
where cold stones roll
beneath bare soles

stare, trace white
foam spilling left to right
without end, its frill

trailed along flapping kelp
gifting iodine bounty
to deep inhaled rhythms –

everyone does this: stands
lonely, longing for something
unremembered, a swaying

in womb-fluid, pulse music,
some relic of becoming,
I am. Or: fingering one's neck,

where arches, slits and pouches
once grooved the embryo's pharynx,
a finned ancestor prompts

some cell recall from before
the tribe unfolded, ripened,
crept from the ooze, and blinked.

Wet to the ankles, bend down,
pick up a pebble and roll it
between thumb and little finger.

COSMIC TIME

Waves heave, swell,
pause, hold breath and
let go in climax,
a tumult of pebbles.
Curls of spume frill,
zip up the tide line.

Wet sands expand.
It is full moon tonight,
at around zenith
yipping foxes will come.
Later, some rooster will yell
at a streak of rose in the sky.

Low winter sun
eases its pale disc
onto Wicklow hills,
fingers grow numb,
the dog folds in on himself.
A chevron of Brent geese
trembles along the horizon
to rest at Bull Island.
A slow heron flaps in to roost.

The heart contracts, rests.
Breaths flow in, out,
almost in time with waves
whose sounds are all consonants

trailing into hisses.
Spring tide ebbs.
Shadow advances.
World rolls.

A train shatters the moment,
Greenwich time its servant.
Just for now though,
clock's artifice is put away,
all the senses heed
light and shadow and tide,
hunger and chilling skin.

Yesterday, parting friends
settled on the next
gathering to happen when
daffodils come into bloom.

LOVE POTION

Here, at the margin where endless wavelets
lick at pebbles, a place to ponder
odds against self aware existence:
say, one particular afternoon
one sperm outswam two hundred million,
rushed headlong into *that* very egg;
scamper up history's mesh of branches,
great greats doubling for each generation,
what if they never met, loved, mated,
but they did – climb back six million years
to the common mother of humans and chimps,
past hairy swingers of canopy,
three hundred and sixty million more years
and a tetrapod leaves its rows of marks
in mud, now stone of Valentia island;
and fish, their gill bones our legacy.
Unwind to single-celled organisms,
first strings of molecules replicating –

so, I am of limpet, of crab, of sole,
of plunging gannets, of wet eyed seals'
suspirations from sun-flecked sea,
lifting to clouds interwoven with vapours
of all the departed.
                              This life is the only
one I can know, granted to me.
I wind up discarded plastic tangles
of fishing line with dangling hooks,
for the bin. I touch my bequeathed philtrum.

Part 5

above plum blossoms
into alto cirrus clouds
three buzzards plait squeals

CORNCRAKE

Crex crex

Stripey jester,
buff and rufous
grasses skulker,
secret hay breaster,

continents-crossing
summer harbinger:
crek-crek crek-crek
crek-crek crek-crek

unharmonious
nocturne grater,
comb dragger
on matchbox striker,

westward dwindling
creaking soothsayer:
mechanization
your steely passport

into thin air.

IN A WOMAN'S SKIN

She's an odd bird, that one,
not altogether here,
but stands, poised on stilts
at the edge of an elsewhere

waiting, with focussed stare,
patient, utterly still,
until, backlit by sun
she seems to shape shift from

some cranky hunched nun
to javelin with scapulars,
then stirs, more silent than breath,
withdraws and kinks her neck,

levitates over the willows,
floats on her broad arched wings,
two stick legs trailing after,
slow flapping, celestial, until

she scrapes the whole marsh sky
with a harsh screeched 'kaark',
lands by the brink of a pool,
her keen yellow round eye

looking both out and in,
minding a time, it is said,
when her plumes were woman skin
in fine silks and purple wool.

At twilight, the white full moon
guides her way back to an oak
to roost among her own kind,
crossed over, returned to this world.

NORTH WEST TRENDS

It is right to hoard certain books.
My battered 1970 Guide
to Birds of Britain and Europe, displays
breeding ranges and wintering grounds
on maps shaded in pink and blue.

The Glossy Ibis, my newest joy,
bred in the 1970s
in Iran, Iraq, Syria, Turkey
and Northern Italy. Now it breeds
in Spain, France, parts of Britain,
with rare sightings in our wetlands.

I found one in a Westmeath bog,
prodding its long sickle bill
in a bright pool, feeling for food.
The bird was all elliptical curve
and delicate swerve of slender neck.
Backlit, it seemed all black, but then
hints of purple-brown iridescence,
and greenish shimmers on the wings
prompted reflection on its name.

One finger tracing my thumbnail maps,
I could probe these North West trends.
Always there will be wandering,
flux, exodus, odyssey,
populations threading their paths
across the atlas of flight and need,
impelled by hope, the urge for life.

Enough for me to watch the Glossy
Ibis poke about in water,
resplendent, knowing I was there
no doubt, and not minding at all.

SWIFTS

Do you remember swifts in multitudes long ago,
stitching the sky at sunset with silver squeal
    needles?

Their shrill pitch pierced through skin, bone and
    brain,
hinting, with scent of privet, syringa and
    buddleia,

the holidays are near, summer spreads ahead,
careless as you lying there supine on a green lea ...

to trace one dodging bird impossible, dozens
    swooping,
shifting like swarms of gnats, gulping myriad
    midges

and as the first stars appeared, the swifts' shrill
    pipes
erased cares of exams, our eyelids half closed ...

those were hours free from worry, without regrets
    or plans,
we were the sum of our senses, we drowsed or
    dreamt we flew.

We used to forecast rain if swifts swung close to
    ground,
glad if they circled thermals higher, becoming
    mere specks.

We always welcomed the migrants back home
   from Africa,
whizzing straight to their nooks in colonies under
   our eaves.

How would it feel to never touch the earth from
   year
to year, then only to cling to a wall to feed your
   young,

to mate on the wing, to rise thousands of metres
   at dusk,
sleep with one half of your brain alert to slow
   down drifting?

we drifted down to slumber with dew cooling our
   brows,
one half of our brains absorbed in screaming
   parties of swifts,

insinuating high notes into the depths of our
   minds,
lifting us to sublimity, stitching us to love.

TREASURE

In a soggy Kilbogget field
Brent geese pace about,
uttering hollow grunts,
periscope necks alert;
away with them as one,
a chevron on swift wings
they press for the estuary.

They came at gold leaf time,
when shorter, darker days
stirred an urge to fly south
from Arctic Canada,
guided by magnetism,
by moon and stars, or who knows,
by spirit guides in the sky …

their cacks cast on the grass
like firm little cigars
are all that they've left, and one
breast feather of sepia,
its vane fringed with down,
its tip a Chinese white,
for me to keep, with thanks.

HIGH JINKS

Exuberance of crows –
a hundred maybe – mount
thermals above the hill.
The blotchy juveniles
test their first year pinions
in cloud-shredding squalls.

They look like jagged gloves
tossed at grey cumulus.
Some fold in their wings,
gyre in screwing plunge,
tumble out from tackles,
one bird shoogles backwards!

Each bird clutches an acorn,
and, passed from claw to beak,
hurls it out in an arc,
plummets earthwards in stoop,
outpaces it, beaks it in,
repeats the trick again –

They practise, control, roll
lightly in swinging dances
with unpredictable gusts;
they must be laughing above
the yellow oaks, scribbling
their ecstasy on the sky.

SING

This year, after my garden robins establish a loving bond,
there comes arctic air. Confused by Nature's prank, he
abandons her and sings lustily, soon attracting a new fancy
bird and they flirt. Robin-lady number one is alone, loveless.
What is to be done?
She sings. Softly, to herself or her god, she sings. She hopes
that warmer days when spring properly arrives will bring
him to his senses and he will return to feed his first love.

in the next door yard
she pegs out washing for one –
sure can sing the blues

KESTREL

pocaire gaoithe

In a northern gale, chin tucked to chest
I gain the brow of Telegraph hill
then stop. I lift up my eyes to blue –
in sky nearby an indifferent hawk
beats the wind, all pinions flouncing
like ardent oarsmen battling a tempest;
'contre jour', every buff feather
gyrates to its own singular plan,
sunbeams glinting between the vanes;
the tail not fanned as in quiet air
but like a lath, the whole arrangement
united in purpose – to fix the head –
steady, poised like an image made,
dark hooked beak brimmed by yellow,
'catch light' mirrored in his round black eye.

The hover is mastered. All below
is shifting though – whins lurch, dry leaves
spin in mad jigs – whose eye could trace
a quivery mouse or piss trails in mulch?
But the spectrum gifted to a kestrel's sight
is forbidden to me. Rheumy eyed
I brace the gusts, stagger on.

ON THE BRINK

Here, on the tidal fringe
over a drystone wall
crek-*crek*, crek-*crek*, crek-*crek*

double-syllabic creaks,
one per second to match
my heart – lub-*dup*, lub-*dup*.

Echoes, or answers, come
from cliffs beyond a gate,
fooling my searching eyes.

Hidden in damp meadow
he crakes through starlit grass,
beaking his one-note grates

as though his chicks depend
on such rasps – and they do –
pleas to plundering blades,

mow *late*, mow *late,* mow *late.*
Let them ride out summer
safe in a shrinking ark,

out on the western edge
where the old farmers nod,
minding summers gone by.

EARTH IS DIMINISHED

Little sunlit wing
like a sail upraised
right angle to a stain,
primary feathers fanned
in last leave taking
on the road's fast lane,
shivers in the blast
as a truck slams past.

Smashed into dust
the eyes that flashed light
from a downy round head;
gone the dawn song,
beak and needle bones
spin in some tyre tread,
the particles broadcast;
she never flew so fast.

Part 6

lambs gambol –
surrounding hills echo
consonants and vowels

SILENCE

What is silence, anyway?
It is hardly ever complete,
absence of wrong noise maybe
or a way of consigning such
to almost irrelevance –

attentive listening then,
to small, kind sounds
emphasizes silence,
like down by the calm lake
when reflections are near perfect,

there are tiny lapping wavelets,
occasional moorhen bubble calls,
and my dog, with dripping beard,
gazes right into my eyes
and, together, we notice.

DRAGONFLY

Once he breathed with gills,
jaws cramped on fish
until days grew longer
and warmer, hormones fizzed,
magic metamorphosed him
into a dragonfly –
a brightly coloured, shining
aerobatic wonder
whose beauty was never made
for human appreciation.

He quartered his pool above
the heads of tetrapods,
among luxuriant ferns,
conifers, horsetails, mosses,
beneath Western skies.

Humming, hunting, mating,
he was majesty of air;
blue sky, sun, clouds,
midges, dragonfly
pretenders to his patch,
his own reflected image,
entered myriad lenses
in his colossal eyes.

After some few weeks
his astonishing body,
its dark, noble chest,
long, horizontal wings

with light-catching windows
framed by pleats of veins,
floated back to nature,
was pressed down, down
in carboniferous mud,
waited out the licks
of warm, tropical seas
and shifting shapes of lands,
ice ages, cosmic blinks.

The grey stone splits,
and in its quiet heart
three hundred million years,
a sleeping dragonfly.

TO A BEE

Bee, your benign hum, as heavy you swing from
    cowslips,
climb apple blossoms, merry-making borage,
dandelions and comfrey, is the very music of life.

Maybe you know this, following your ancient
    imperative
sipping your nectar; you need to fly from flower
    to flower,
shoogling cuckoo spit insects in their May bubble
    dreams,

your little leg baskets brimming with yellow
    pollen
for larvae, planning for vitality of your kind,
the young bees you won't see by next month

for exhausted you will die, will have fulfilled
    your life.
How can you know, bee saver, that the cleverest
    of animals
who cannot crack your secrets, depend utterly on
    you?

They fret in counting houses, smartly spray
    toxins
on all healing herbs starring the old land
rapidly nudging bees to a dwindling past tense.

Happily, you, unaware, brush your golden hairs
with pollen, bringing grains to welcoming female
parts.
I pass a finger over your furry cape for luck.

THE TOAD

I like to flip up stones
to find what I may smell
and feel, deeper down.
On shelly Uig dunes
where Lewis chessmen lay
for seven hundred years,
a piece of pinkish gneiss
asks to be upturned.

There squats a bumpy toad
with hips and knees all flexed,
toes and fingers spread,
engaged in inner work.
I return his darkness.
He may be there still
in his Berie Sands hole,
seeing truth, clear as day.

LIKE A MAN

Look, he's smiling at me, like a human!
Running my fingers through the thick, lanolated pile of
ram's wool with its distinctive unwashed scent, I can see his
lip curl up, and the corners of his mouth lift like an ad for
dentures.

the ram's tight wool
smells of animal and grease -
what does the ram sniff?

You demolish my anthropomorphism. You say, 'He is flaring
his nostrils which elevates his upper lip. He is sniffing you,
checking if you are in oestris.'

HETERODOXY

Over a coffee
Theosony you offered -
God sound, like theology
is God talk -
Gregorian chant
I think you meant,
maybe psalm singing,
hymning with praise;

I thought of a blackbird
fluting its vesper,
all of the sounds
that catch the heart
before the brain:
rhythms of air
in a swan's wings
over the loch;

lapping waves,
beech leaves whispering,
bumble bees drowsing
on spindle flowers
calming thought-chatter
with moments of Mind
making a listener
pause, grateful.

SPELL

It was my custom to call at the gate,
Horsey, Horsey, and straightaway would hear
hollow deep hammering hooves in the woods,
and you would appear with nostrils flared
inhaling me, sharing your grassy breath,
my veiled image there in your trusting eyes,
your loose velvet lower lip cupped in my palm,
white star on your Amazon-veined bay head
whose relaxed load you would lay on my neck
and with one hock flexed, eyes closed, you slept.

When you didn't arrive and I asked round about,
they said, gone to England – since then I have
      thought
how easy it is to be jolted by change.
Unbolted, the rusty gate tilts from one hinge.

Part 7

swarm of honey bees
settle on a rowan tree –
the day sweetens

O EUROPE!

A boy crosses borders
alone in the host,
in white heat parched
he dreams of folding
his limbs in blue shade
of acacia or canvas,
of supping from springs
in his cool cupped palms

but gullies are dry
as his lips and tongue,
no trees or tents
to screen midday sun,
he dares not rest
in heat that shimmers
mirages in the desert
where his torn shoes push

to the sea he imagines
he will sail across
to a life with no guns
in distant lands
where there must be trees
to climb in green shade:
he whispers again,
'I am not afraid'.

ABOUT ANGELS

some things angels have not:
pockets
grudges
opposable thumbs
knowledge of good and harm

where you might find one:
edges
periphery of vision
by water
near trees
by a man's heart
in his sleeping bag in the city

why they may be here:
to save us from pride
shame
grasping
to lift us from griefs
tramping beside us on the way
to remind us to play
and to be still when they repose

how they might manifest:
in many forms and always lofty
an aura about other angels
wings if they possess wings
are invisible
as natural as leaves
but like rainbows they stitch together

Heaven and Earth
bright eyed
mighty chested
to hold great hearts
and usually you will find
a drip slips slowly
from their noses

DEVELOPMENT

In my hut there are many bowls.
Some are marked by moulds in splits.
Ancestors' ones are fragile fossils.

At equinox we fill one with liquor,
pass hand to hand, sup and give thanks
for bounty; it has always been thus.

It is our custom for every mother
to make a bowl for each new baby.
This honours the form of a woman's pelvis.

I squat in the leafy shade, and sing.
I turn my piece of wood and whittle
with hope a bowl for my waking child,

a bundle as light as a fruit on my back;
her own grandchild should feed from the hollow
scooped out and oiled by its great grandmother.

What can you feel through my body, Child?
I sense roots tearing, the thump of trunks.
Can you hear rip saws, tree spirits' shrieks?

What do you smell? Our forest burns;
do you see birds falling out of the sky,
on a spreading bare black patch of earth?

What now for the forest's gifts we share –
for shelter, clothing, foods and cures,
tools and honey and blessed rain?

PASSAGE

Walls of concrete, walls of steel,
the greatest problem for the world –
exclusion of the poor and ill.

In an Irish wall the gap is king,
all sprinkles of light and windy tunes,
storm resistant, a genius thing.

Cobbles were gleaned from fields, then flats,
knit one upright, purl one step,
v-shaped notches to pass and repass.

Mercurial stoats dance through holes,
wild goats balance on shifting tops,
pine martens sniff for shrews and voles.

The crispy lichen mats on stones
were gathered in for crocks of dye
by children scraping walls with spoons.

A *meitheal* repairs, true to arts
of ancestors, with song and story;
kids crack swollen hazel nuts.

In limestones, myriad fossils whorl
bedded for aeons out of mind
from tropical sea to Burren wall.

Now occupied by chalky snails
the shady nooks abuzz with bees,
where wild thyme grows and blue harebells

wave with fragrant lady's bedstraw,
herb Robert, orchids and navelwort,
the birds well fed by hip and haw.

Lone trees are bent by westerlies
and clouds fling shadows on the stones
hand-placed in lines like field rosaries.

Rumbles of slippage, always movement,
rained on or silvered by moonlight, this wall
invites much crossing: gaps are paramount.

A FIRST WORLD PIQUE

I could patter
up sheer walls,
dazzling windows,
scoot across ceilings
like Kafka's insect,
could peg along
the lower surface
of the tilted glass
convention centre,
upon my sticky
gecko soles,
congealed with spat-
out bubble gums,
which have hitched
their evil rides
from pocked pavements,
filthy accretions
cleaving between
rubber notches
on newest shoes.
In a wax,
I pluck reluctant
feet, whose tacky
kisses distract
from traffic hazards,
alluring shops,
people begging
without shelter.

WINGS

his gaunt limbs curl
on a cardboard mat
one eye half open

the full moon caresses him
pressed in a doorway
he half hears drunks roar

his half awake brain
implores the moon
to bring gold dream wings

he will drift away
as a swift over Dublin
away to a green place

on Mount Latmos, say,
to tend his sheep
nearer to the moon

whose beams make silver
the pillows of kings -
who brings a street sleeper

gold wings